IT'S A GIRL!

– An ante-natal comedy for the nuclear age with a cappella music.

It's A Girl! is an account by five women from 'Bradstow' of how they had their first babies together and at the same time took part in the town's fight to stop a nuclear dump being built on its doorstep.

'superbly funny . . . the heart of the piece is in the interplay (and some wonderful a cappella harmonising) between the five friends.'

Brian Morton, *London Evening Standard*

IT'S A GIRL!

A Play by John Burrows

with a cappella music
by Andy Whitfield

Methuen Drama

METHUEN YOUNG DRAMA

First published in Great Britain in 1988
by Methuen Drama, A division of OPG Services Ltd,
Michelin House, 81 Fulham Road, London SW3 6RB
Distributed in the United States of America
by HEB Inc., 70 Cork Street, Portsmouth, New Hampshire 03801.
John Burrows *It's A Girl!* copyright © 1988 Music copyright ©
1988 Andy Whitfield

Printed and bound in Great Britain by
Cox & Wyman Ltd, Reading

British Library Cataloguing in Publication Data

Burrows, John
  It's a girl! an ante-natal comedy for
  the nuclear age.
  I. Title   II. Whitfield, Andy
  822'.914

  ISBN 0-413-19090-0

To Anna

It's A Girl! was commissioned by The Dukes Theatre, Lancaster, and given its first performance on 25th February 1987, with the following cast (the characters from the play-within-the-play are in brackets):

MARY	Stephanie Sales
CELIA	Nicola Sloane
MINA	Julie Battie
LINDA	Jane Nash
EVE	Liza Spenz

Directed by John Burrows
Musical direction by Andy Whitfield
Choreographed by Kiki Gale
Designed by Alice Purcell

The production subsequently toured England and Scotland and opened at the Bush Theatre, London on 27th November 1987 with the following cast:

MARY	Stephanie Sales
CELIA	Nicola Sloane
MINA	Buffy Davis
LINDA	Jane Nash
EVE	Beccy Wright

Production Notes.

1. The first half of the play roughly covers the first three months of Linda's pregnancy. The second half roughly covers the last three months. So the women should have bulges in the second half but not in the first.

2. Everyone should stay on stage for the scenes they're not in and be part of the story being told.

3. All props, including the baby, are mimed.

4. Doubling:
MARY also plays LEN and DEFENDING COUNCIL. CELIA also plays MIDWIFE, NIREX, WOMAN, JACKY and PROSECUTING COUNCIL. MINA also plays MELVYN. And EVE also plays GP, GERRY, JUDGE and MAN.

Author's Note

It's A Girl! is an account by five women from 'Bradstow' of how they had their first babies together and at the same time took part in the town's fight to stop a nuclear dump being built on its doorstep. They tell their story on a bare stage with 'nothing up their sleeves', except a fluid playing style, a little tongue-in-cheek choreography, and a lot of five-part harmony a capella singing.

It is, in a sense, a play within a play. The 'outside' play takes place in real time, is set in whatever theatre the show is being presented in, and asks the audience to pretend the actresses listed in the programme are actually ordinary women from Bradstow who've come to tell their story, in spite of the fact that they can break into five-part harmony at the drop of a hat. The 'inside' play, the story the women tell, takes place over nine months, is set in Bradstow, and further asks the audience to pretend those same ordinary women, without so much as an acting diploma between them, can also play all the characters their story entails.

None of this, of course, will bother the audience. It's no more than the average pantomine demands. The same goes for the presentation techniques the show uses – direct address, asides, songs, comic business, audience participation – they're all the stock-in-trade of low-brow theatre. Of course, if *It's A Girl!* was really just the lightweight romp it pretends to be the intricasies and the inconsistencies of the script wouldn't bother the actors either. But the fact is anyone involved in a production of the play will have to comply with its major requirement: at every point in the performance a difficult balance must be maintained between the comic devices written for entertainment and accessibility on the one hand, and the play's serious content on the other.

It's a fine old juggling act, believe me. All it needs is for the actresses to get a whiff of the liberties the script takes, and a glimpse of the liberties the show must take to work in performance, plus the high of a bit of close harmony singing for the whole thing to go over the top and the truth of the story straight out the window. The antidote is to remember the play's basic premise. Actresses are acting characters acting a story. The yardstick for the production is not what the actresses find funny but what the characters they're playing find funny. And the absolute safety factor here is that however comic they care to make the telling of their story, *the women from Bradstow* will always make certain that its spirit and heroism come shining through.

John Burrows, 1988

JOHN BURROWS is an actor, writer and director. With fellow actor John Harding he has written many plays for their own performance including the largely autobiographical *The Golden Pathway Annual*, and *Loud Reports*, a history of the British Empire with music by Peter Skellern. Among John Burrows' own plays are: *Son of a Gun* (1976 Sidewalk Theatre, UK fringe tour), *Cash Street* (1977 Sidewalk Theatre, UK fringe tour), *Restless Natives* (1978) Albany Empire – music by Rick Lloyd), *Dole Queue Fever* (1978) Albany Empire – music by Rick Lloyd), *Freedom Point* (1979 Albany Empire – music by Rick Lloyd), *One Big Blow* (1980 7:84 Theatre Company, UK and Scandinavian tours, Granada TV – music by Rick Lloyd), and *Wartime Stories* (1984 Drill Hall, London – music by Andrew Dickson).

PART ONE

The women enter and set up music as:

EVE: Ladies and gentlemen, tonight, live on stage, a group of
young women brought together by the miracle of childbirth,
the Bradstow Regain-Your Shape-After Pregnancy Coffee
Circle!
Music swells.
For those of you wondering: the kids are at home with their
fathers. And it really is unbelievably wonderful to be here or
anywhere tonight without them. Thank you for making it all
possible. Of course, any time we're not on stage we will be
'phoning home just to be on the safe side. So don't worry, we
do feel pretty guilty being up here enjoying ourselves.
Music swells.

Ladies and gentlemen, can we introduce ourselves? We
are . . . the refined Celia! . . . Eccentric Mary! . . . our
resident ecologist, Mina The Green! . . . and the heroine of
our story tonight, the lovely Linda! . . . And of course, the
one who lost the draw and has to do the introduction, yours
truly, the ever-so-slightly extrovert, Eve!
Music swells.
Now ladies and gentlemen, Bradstow! I'm sure you all
remember it . . . One of the places the Government wanted to
put a nuclear dump, or depository for low level radioactive
waste as they say in polite circles. It never happened, I'm
pleased to say. They dropped the idea just before the election
on account of the cost: we threatened to vote Labour. Ladies
and gentlemen, the Bradstow Regain-Your-Shape-After-
Pregnancy-Coffee Circle stands before you tonight as members
of the minute band of individuals who can claim to have made
our leader change her mind . . . Not only mothers but also
political giant killers!
Music swells.
So there we are, ladies and gentlemen, a story of Childbirth
and Parliamentary Democracy. Or in other words, Sex and
Violence – you can't get away from it, can you?! Okay, let's
put you in the picture. Originally from up north, our heroine
and her husband got on their bike – their tandem – and came

to live in Bradstow just a few months before they tried to twin us with Chernobyl and the balloon went up. Ladies and gentlemen by way of getting going a little recap for you now of how Linda moved south, got pregnant, and came to meet us at the clinic!

Music swells and leads into:

A Mythical World Beyond Watford

LINDA: Ee by gum! You've been out of work six months. Melvyn. Life's hard here in the north of England.

MELVYN: Nay, Linda, love. I've found a job.

LINDA: There's nowt round this way.

MELVYN: No, down south! I treated meself to a pennorth of chips and saw it in newspaper.

LINDA: Oh, Melvyn, a new start! Good job we bought council house. We can sell up and go anywhere.

MELVYN: Aye, lass, money we get for this place, we'll have a new pair of clogs each, hire hand-cart for furniture, and leg it down A1 behind Jarrow Marchers.

MELVYN: Well, here we are, Linda, love. The sunny south! And there's where going to live. What d'you think?

LINDA: Oh, Melvyn, it's wonderful! Me own little house, all lovely and new!

MELVYN: They don't come newer than that, Linda, love. This time yesterday it were still in its box! No, hang on, that is the box. That's the house next to it in pieces. That's real wood, that is. You can tell by the leaves!

LINDA: Oh, can we go inside, Melvyn?

MELVYN: They've only just started building it, Linda, love. You can wait a quarter of an hour, surely!

LINDA: Oh Melvyn, it's fantastic! It must have cost the earth!

MELVYN: Aye, it did! But you earn more down here, don't you? I've worked it out, after everything, we'll still have a bit left over each month.

LINDA: I love you!

MELVYN: And if some months we want to eat we'll just increase mortgage.

LINDA: I wonder what bedrooms are like?

MELVYN: I love it when you talk dirty!

LINDA: How were it for you?

MELVYN: Great! How were it for you?

LINDA: Great! It started in me toes, crept up me thighs, then me bum sort of glowed and went wobbly.

MELVYN: Well, you know what they say love.

LINDA: Aye, there's nowt like an electric blanket!

MELVYN: It's like a dream come true. Good job! Nice house! Lovely wife!

LINDA: There's only one thing missing.

MELVYN: What's that?

LINDA: A baby. D'you think we're doing it right?

MELVYN: I would have thought so.

LINDA: I mean d'you think we're getting the nuts and bolts of it right, Melvyn?

MELVYN: I would have thought the nut and bolt were fine, love.

LINDA: Why can't I get pregnant then?

GP: It's very difficult to say, Mrs Bragg. There are all sorts of tubes that could be blocked. Your vaginal excretions could be killing Mr Bragg's sperms. Mr Bragg might not be producing any sperms – his testicles might be too hot.

MELVYN: We have bought an electric blanket.

GP: It could be a factor.

MELVYN: We put it on before we go to bed but we always turn it off before we make love.

LINDA: We have it off all night.

GP: What sort d'you have? Under or over?

MELVYN: Well, what would you say, Linda? It's mostly me on top really, isn't it?

LINDA: Does it make any difference, Doctor?

GP: I'm going to refer you to a specialist, Mr and Mrs Bragg.

LINDA: Melvyn, you know how we're supposed to be going to specialist next week.

MELVYN: Aye.

LINDA: I think it might be waste of time.

MELVYN: If he's anything like that doctor I wouldn't be at all surprised.

LINDA: No, I don't mean that. I mean I think it might have happened anyway.

MELVYN: Oh my god!

LINDA: What's the matter?

MELVYN: I'm not sure I'm ready to be a father.

LINDA: Well, I don't know what you think you've been playing at! This bed's not seen a pyjama bottom in months!

MELVYN: Have you seen Doctor?

LINDA: I've been once. I've got to go back. He'll let me know one way or the other . . . I thought Patrick if it's a boy. And if it's a girl, Natasha.

GP: Well, Mrs Bragg, I don't know specifically how. But you definitely are. Congratulations!

I've Done It

I've done it
I've done it
I've done it
I've done it

I've done it
I'm gonna be a mum
I've fallen
Me oven's got a bun.

I've made it
Linda's in the club
I'm going to swell up
Like a washing tub

I've done it
A woman's greatest thing

I'm expecting
I'll give me mam a ring.

She'll love it
She's gonna be a gran
I know
She's already bought the baby's pram

I'm gonna have a baby
I'm full of hopes and fears
I'm waiting now
For something pretty big
I suppose it means I'm lumbered
For years and years and years
A little kid, a little kid,
A little kid, god forbid
It might have Melvyn's ears.

I've done it
I'm really overjoyed
I'm easy
If it's a girl or a boy.

I've done it
It's made me life complete
Don't know why but I
Am crying in the street

What a feeling
It's great to be alive
I'm caring
For someone else inside

I've done it
I've reproduced me kind
Well I will have done
In under nine months time.

I don't care who's listening
Don't care if I'm a bore
I don't care if
The world goes bang
I don't care about nothing
Not bothered any more
I've been to see the doctor
I've just found out for sure
I've done it

EVE's *house*.

EVE: Mina stuck a notice on the board outside the Post Office, saying Mum-to-be Circle starting and this lot turned up!

CELIA: The idea, is, Linda that we meet each week in a different person's house. And it's rather nice!

MARY: When am I doing it?

CELIA: I haven't got a clue, lovey. Mina's the big chief! She's gotthe list.

MINA: Celia, I'm not the Chief. I just got the group together, that's all. And there isn't a list. It's alphabetical, Mary. Eve the first week, Celia the second, then you, then me.

CELIA: Sounds like a list to me.

MARY: Wouldn't it be easier with a list?

CELIA: I certainly think so.

EVE: Mary, there is a list, sort of. Every fourth week it's you, okay? That's all you've got to remember.

MARY: I thought paté with french bread – some of that uncooked dough mix that you do yourself, that's quite nice – with a small individual green salad each, and filter coffee. I don't think we want wine do we, lunchtime? Few cans of Carlsberg, p'raps. I prefer it actually.

MINA: We shouldn't really be drinking alcohol at all, should we. It all crosses the placenta.

MARY: No, it's got a Danish name but they brew it in this country now.

CELIA: Except that now Linda's joined us, it won't be every fourth week it'll be every fifth week, won't it?

MINA: I'll let you know the week beforehand, Mary.

EVE: So who's not had a think about my aerobics idea, then? Little work-out each week . . . A bop a day to keep the stretch marks away!

MINA: I think I'd prefer something more gentle, more natural somehow.

EVE: Like what?

MINA: Well, I don't know. something yoga based.

CELIA: Or perhaps even 'chat' based.

MINA: What do you think, Mary?

MARY: I was just wondering, if we met in the pub each week, we wouldn't have to have a list, would we?

MINA: You can't really do relaxation exercises or aerobics in a pub, can you?

MARY: No but there's darts and pool and you can have a little glass of something. That can be quite relaxing, I find.

CELIA: Look, can I put my cards on the table? I've come to this motherhood lark late in life. No, let me rephrase that, latish . . . a little later in life than most, and frankly, whether we swing from the chandaliers, or get pissed in a pub or meditate in a field, to me its irrelevant. What I've got to have, to have this baby, is moral support. So can we somehow do that, please?

MINA: Oh, absolutely bloody wonderfully well put, Celia! I couldn't agree more.

MARY: I've got the new Mothercare catalogue. Gerry gets it earlier because of his job.

CELIA: Is he in publishing?

MARY: No, he's an estate agent.

EVE: So where does that leave the aerobics?

MARY: He reckons none of the big houses are selling.

CELIA: Really? Why's that?

MARY: Because of this dump . . .

EVE: No-one wants to live here any more, Celia.

CELIA: I don't know why you're taking that attitude. I'm not in favour of the blasted thing. I just don't think we should behave like members of the National Union of Mineworkers to demonstrate the point.

EVE: All I did was ask you to come to a meeting in the village hall about it. Not join the IRA.

MARY: They've got a lovely little knitted continental all-in-one suit in it. Reversible in pink and blue. So, whatever you have, boy or girl, you can turn it inside out and use it for either. It's really quite classy, Celia, you'd like it.

EVE: How does being an estate agent get you the Mothercare

catalogue earlier?

MARY: Gerry's sister is the assistant manager.

MINA: I think it's absolutely criminal! They want to dig up 500 acres of airfield. Spend fifty years filling it with radio-active waste. Then get us to live on top of it for another 300 years while it decays.

EVE: I mean that must be worth a little bit of fuss, surely, Celia?

CELIA: I don't want contractors' lorries going past the end of my drive any more than you do, Mina!

MINA: Well, I haven't got a drive, actually, Celia, I've just got a little front garden, but I do grow vegetables in it, organically if possible, which I certainly don't want choked with petrol fumes, so I do take your point. But, more important, surely, if all this stuff leaks out and gets into the water supply, or if the background radiation goes up, what happens then? To us and our children? It's frightening!
Everyone considers this.

MARY: I think you just have to be philosophical and not think about it.
Everyone considers this.

CELIA: Where do you stand on all this, Linda?

LINDA: I'm not sure. I didn't really know anything about it till now.

MINA: How near to the airfield d'you live?

LINDA: I live just over the way from it on the new estate. you can see it out me top window.

CELIA: There's been one hell of houhaa about it.

LINDA: I suppose I've been trying to get pregnant.

> *Sitting in the Clinic*
> Sitting in the clinic
> Waiting to be seen
> In and out the toilet
> The seventh time I've been
> Being pregnant's so much fun
> Life is nicer as a nun

Vaginal irritation
Flatulence
And constipation
Are complaints
The pregnant woman
Can't avoid

Sickness in the morning
Moods and crying
Without warning
And don't forget
That itchy twitchy
Haemorrhoid
Yes being pregnant's so much fun
Life is nicer as a nun.

Sitting in the clinic
Waiting in the line
Where's the bloody doctor
Christ he takes his time
We've read all the magazines
Honey, Queen and Seventeen

Falling down and fainting
A back that's nearly
Always aching
Remind a girl
That motherhood's
A thing divine

Sore breasts and hypertension
Swollen veins
And indigestion
But apart from
That we're
Absolutely fine
'Cos being pregnant's so much fun
Life is nicer as a nun.

Sitting in the clinic
Waiting to be called
Reading all the posters
Covering the walls.
Don't have X-rays, clean your teeth
Give up smoking, wear a sheath.

Ankles that are puffy
Cramp and phelgm
If you're unlucky
Would you like
To hear about my
Bleeding gums
Aching feet and stretch marks
Feeling wacked
Before the day starts
Why does anybody
Choose to be
A mum
'Cos being pregnant's so much fun
Life is nicer as a nun.
Let's all become one
Amen.

LINDA *is lying on her back. The* GP *is performing a vaginal examination. The* MIDWIFE *is helping.*

GP: We do it for a number of reasons, Mrs Bragg. . . . To confirm that the size of the uterus is in agreement with the suggested duration of the pregnancy; to ensure that the pregnancy is normal; to exclude the presence of any infection or abnormality; to assess the size of the pelvis. It's pretty standard on the first visit. Lovely . . . Fine!
He's finished and sets about taking his gloves off. The MIDWIFE *takes over.*

MIDWIFE: Okay, Mrs Bragg, doctor's done. That's tremendous! You can put your pants on again now.

GP: So how are you feeling, Mrs Bragg? How have you been?

LINDA: Why, is there something wrong, Doctor?

GP: Not that I'm aware of. It's all pretty straightforward from my point of view. Unless you've got any problems.

LINDA: No, I'm quite happy, thank you.

GP: Don't be afraid to ask questions, when you come. Jot them down on a piece of paper and either I or Sister MacWhinney will do our best to answer them. Not too many. There's always a lot of you ladies in this condition. Somehow we have to find time to see you all. Now, where would you like to have this baby of yours?

LINDA: Well, I've been thinking about it, doctor, and I would like to have it at home.

GP: No, you misunderstand me, Mrs Bragg. I mean where in the sense of which hospital.

LINDA: I don't want to have it in hospital.

GP: Why's that?

LINDA: I just don't.

GP: It's not much of a reason, Mrs Bragg, medically speaking.

LINDA: Me mother had all of us at home.

GP: I don't think it's a good idea to resurrect the obstetric practices of the north of England from a quarter-of-a-century ago, really, do you?

LINDA: It seemed to work all right.

GP: It's like a lot of things, we've moved on. I mean you wouldn't be very happy if we were still operating without anaesthetic, would you?

LINDA: No.

GP: The prime consideration is the safety of you and your child. This is your first child. We don't know what's going to happen. All the evidence points to hospital confinement being safer than home confinement. A woman having her baby in hospital can have complete and absolute confidence that everything is being done to guarantee the health and safety of herself and her child.

LINDA: You see I don't feel that.

GP: Well then you're being very arrogant and silly, Mrs Bragg.

LINDA: No, I don't think so. Everything today is supposed to be for our own good. But more often than not it doesn't seem to work out that way, does it. Me mother'll come down. I would just like my baby to come into the world without any interference from anyone . . . you asked me where I want to have it and I've told you. Now as far as I'm concerned that's all there is to it.

MIDWIFE: You're crying now, Mrs Bragg, but you'd cry a lot more if Doctor were to say yes and baby died.

LINDA: I don't need a lecture from some childless bloody spinster thank you very much! Is he gonna help me or not?!

GP: No. I'm not Mrs Bragg. I'm not prepared to take responsibility for such a selfish course of action. It's not what motherhood's about.

LINDA: How do you know?

LINDA's *bedroom*.

LINDA: Melvyn!

MELVYN: Yes, Linda, love?

LINDA: I should like to make love.

MELVYN: Is that wise, Linda?

LINDA: What you talking about?

MELVYN: You know, in your condition.

LINDA: It's perfectly all right. I've looked in book.

MELVYN: No don't disturb little bugger! He might be having a kip. He won't want a great big thingy popping in and out banging him on the back of the head, will he?

LINDA: I think you better look at this book, Melvyn, it doesn't quite work like that. Women's bodies aren't hollow you know. I've not rented a room out to a little person. And I'm afraid however big you like to think your thingy is, inside the womb he won't feel a thing.

MELVYN: How comes?

LINDA: Well for one thing, according to book, he's 1.3 cms long at the moment and he's hardly got a brain.

MELVYN: Will he look like me as well?

LINDA: I see, so you've got me pregnant and that's that, is it?

MELVYN: I don't see the point. You've got a full tank, you want me to squeeze in an extra gallon . . .

LINDA: Nine months of nothing, I see. Where's Mr Hot Balls gone that's what I want to know?

MELVYN: Oh come on, then . . .

LINDA: No, I'm not bothered now. I've lost it.

MELVYN: Oh, fair enough, night, night, Linda love. See you in morning . . .

She starts to cry.
Don't be daft, I'm only joking.
She won't let him comfort her.
I was joking! What's the matter?

LINDA: I went to the clinic today. It was terrible.

MELVYN: Why?

LINDA: They asked me where I want to have the baby.

MELVYN: What's so terrible about that?

LINDA: Nothing.

MELVYN: So why was it terrible then?

LINDA: I said I wanted to have it at home. They didn't want to know.

MELVYN: Didn't you explain? I'm giving up me job. We're moving into caravan. And you're having baby behind gas works.

LINDA: I'm serious, Melvyn. I've thought about it. I'm going to have the baby here. In this bed!
MELVYN *leaps up.*

MELVYN: What the bloody hell are you talking about, woman? You can't have a baby in a bed like this!

LINDA: Why not?

MELVYN: Because there's nothing medical about it! It's not even orthopaedic! Supposing something goes wrong!

LINDA: Like what?

MELVYN: What is going on with you?! I can't keep up! You're going potty.

LINDA: The majority of births are fine until the doctors get hold of you.

MELVYN: Where's it all coming from, that's what I wanna know? You're like a bloody different person!

LINDA: Put something on, Melvyn! It's ridiculous arguing with you with nothing on!

MELVYN: No I bloody won't! What's the matter?! You've seen it all before.

LINDA: I know, but street hasn't! I've not lined the curtains yet.
He sits down immediately

MELVYN: Linda, I know when you're pregnant you can go a

bit strange but . . . honest, love, you can't go this strange. It's not fair on the rest of us.

LINDA: Who you talking about? There's only you and me. We don't know anybody.

MELVYN: Is that what the trouble is? Are you lonely? What about these other girls you've met, having babies?

LINDA: I feel trapped. I feel helpless. I feel like anyone can do anything and I can't say a thing one way or another. I mean what have I got inside me? I don't know?

MELVYN: You've got a baby inside you! And you've gotta pull yourself together, Linda.

LINDA: I'm just being used. Me whole existence.

MELVYN: I've had enough of this! You can sleep on your bloody own, woman! If it's that much trouble, get rid of it! It's all the same to me!

The mother-to-be circle is lying on the floor.

MINA: And stretch . . . and stretch . . . from the tips of the toes to the top of your head, tense every muscle . . . try and imagine you're stretching yourself from one side of the room to the other . . . feel the tension, behind your knees, along your thighs, particularly clench those very important muscles for us around the anus and the birth canal . . .

CELIA: Oh really, Mina, does it have to be quite so anatomical?

MINA: What would you like me to call them, Celia?

CELIA: I don't want you to call them anything, thank you! Just leave it to me. If I've got it, I'll clench it!

MINA: Keep going! . . . Arch the spine! Flex the chest! . . . Stick out the breasts!

EVE: Wiggle the nipples!

MINA: Distort the face! . . . Make it as ugly as you can!
CELIA *has given up.*

EVE: Celia, that is really grotesque!

MINA: And finally, the arms and the fingers, reach out! . . . and stretch . . . and stretch!

CELIA: Mina, I snapped years ago, darling.

MINA: And relax! . . . Now feel all that tension draining away.
  Trickling away like water. Like the tide returning to the sea.
  And you're lying on a beautiful beach somewhere. Feel the
  hot sand supporting you and the warmth of the sun gently
  kissing your naked body.

CELIA: Oh dear, here we go again.

MINA: And in the distance, if you listen carefully, you can just
  make out the soft cry of sea gulls and the gentle lapping of the
  waves.
  MARY *begins to snore.*
  And very soon every muscle in your body is totally, totally
  relaxed.
  EVE *suddenly writhes in agony.*

LINDA: What's wrong?! What's the matter?!
  EVE *jumps up shouting trying desperately to stamp her foot.*

CELIA: I'm not sure, Linda, but I think this might be aerobics!

MINA: This is ridiculous! One's given up! One's gone to sleep
  and one's leaping around like a moron! We're meant to be
  relaxing for God's sake!

EVE: Cramp is bloody painful, Mina.

CELIA: Mary! . . . wake up!
  MARY *doesn't stir.*
  Come on! . . . We're going to the pub!
  *She instantly snaps out of it without quite knowing where she
  is.*

MARY: Oh, I was having such an erotic dream! When you said
  we were on that beach, Mina, being kissed. It took me right
  back to the honeymoon. We had this whole beach to ourselves
  and we made love half in the water and half out.

CELIA: Which half?

MARY: Well, we couldn't very well have had our heads under
  the water, could we, Celia?

CELIA: Not for an hour-and-a-half, Mary, no.

MARY: We had nothing on . . . Nothing with us . . . Just a few
  cans of beer. It was very very idyllic.

MINA: I've got *one* person doing it properly.

LINDA: Well, I wouldn't say I was doing it properly,
  exactly . . .

MINA: Don't apologise for doing it right, Linda, for God's sake.
LINDA looks devastated.
I'm sorry.
Everyone goes quiet.
Does everyone know about the coach going to lobby
parliament tomorrow. 8 o'clock outside the Church Hall?

EVE: Yep!

CELIA: No, what's this?

MINA: Parliament is debating the special development order
that NIREX has applied for. To start surveying the airfield.
We want to get as many people along as possible to register
our disapproval.

CELIA: It sounds great fun. Do we have to say now?

MINA: It would help.

MARY: I'm going, Celia!

CELIA: Oh well, if you're going Mary, wild horses wouldn't
keep me away.

MARY: I'll fill a hip flask. I love a coach ride.

MINA: What about you, Linda? Can you go?

LINDA: Not tomorrow, no.

MINA: We can't really afford to be apathetic at the moment.

LINDA: I've got someone coming.

MINA: Can't you put them off? I'm sure they won't mind. Who
is it?
LINDA starts to cry.
What's the matter? What are you crying for?

LINDA: If you must know I've got the midwife coming.

EVE: Mina, I can't stand this, you're being horrible.

MINA: Is something wrong, Linda?

LINDA: No, I've just decided to have my baby at home, that's
all. And they want to see where I live. If it wasn't for that, I
would definitely be coming, Mina.

MINA: I didn't think you could have your first baby at home.

LINDA: Well, I wrote to this place that supports home
confinements and apparently you can. The woman there wrote
me back a letter and told me what to do.

She brings out the letter.
I carry it around with me. It's wonderful.
MINA *takes it and reads the first paragraph.*

MINA: It is . . . I think, you should read it out.
She hands the letter back.

LINDA: It's pretty long.

MINA: Never mind.

EVE: Go on, Lin, read it out!

LINDA: I know it off by heart.

Dear Linda Bragg, as you will see from the top leaflet
you do not need a GP at all and the District Health Authority
must absolutely send you a midwife for ante- and post-natal
care and the delivery in your home. I'm afraid that you will
have to get writing as advised but that is all there is to it.
Your right to midwifery attention is absolute. And if
necessary, and called by a midwife, a GP must turn out for an
emergency. In fact, the midwife would telephone the hospital
emergency facilities for help – they are provided too, despite
what may be admitted to. If necessary the midwife can stitch,
so you need not worry about that. I hope this sets your mind
at ease. The London Birth Centre would advise and support
you but I strongly advise that you do not accept any GP cover
even it seems 'sympathetic' for strategic reasons. We want *all*
doctors to know they are dispensable and they should feel
pleased and honoured to look after their pregnant patients.
They should not do it as a favour. Lots and lots of women are
having babies at home now and the procedure for lining up the
midwife is the same wherever you live. Let me know how you
get on. Best wishes. Catherine White.

Woman's Work

Chorus
We'll go to London
Sort out the government
You stay in Bradstow
Sort out being a mum.

Half-chorus
'Cos there's no clash of ideology

Between politics and biology
'Cos it's all woman's work
And woman's work is never done.

CELIA: I'm down for a hospital birth
It's more my cup of tea
I'm glad you're doing it your way
But rather you than me.

(*Half-chorus.*)

MINA: I'm down for a natural birth
Without the use of drugs
I shall squat down in a corner.
Pretend I'm lifting spuds.

(*Full chorus.*)

MARY: I'm down for a technical birth
With everything they've got
They can knock me out beforehand
And wake me up when it's in its cot.

(*Half-chorus.*)

EVE: I'm down for a quicky
In and out with minimum of fuss
I shall go in at the last minute
And probably have it on the bus.

(*Full chorus.*)

LINDA's *house.*

LINDA: Melvyn, I've arranged to have a home birth. The midwife's been. She's seen everything and it's fine. And that's what I want to do. I just want to feel I can do something about something on me own. On our own, love. Together. I mean they can sack you. Make you move from one end of the country to the other. Even dump a bloody dump on your doorstep, if they want to. Well, just let this be what we want for once, eh? Please.

MELVYN: I don't think it's right, Linda. I don't think it's best. For you or the baby. I don't want to lose you. Either of you.

LINDA: Melvyn, have you ever stopped to think we both come from a very long line of people all of whom were born at home and none of whom died in the process. Me mother had six. One in a prefab. Two in a back to back. And three on the ninteenth floor of a high rise block of flats.

MELVYN: Well, my mother had me and my brother in hospital and she reckons if it hadn't been for the hospital she would have lost David.

LINDA: I'm going to have it at home, Melvyn.

MELVYN: No you're not.

LINDA: It's not up to you. It's my body.

MELVYN: It's my baby. It does take two you know! You're not the Virgin Mary.

LINDA: Well, take it then! If you can look after it for the next nine months, I'll give it to you now.

MELVYN: I won't let them in. I'll change the bloody locks!

LINDA: You do that and I'll have the law on you!

MELVYN: What you talking about? You're my responsibility. In law what I say goes.

LINDA: Oh, yeah, well you read this. You're in for a big surprise!
She gives him the letter.

MELVYN: I don't think so.
He tears it up.

LINDA: You bastard!

MELVYN: Now what you gonna do?

> *Another Woman Goes*
> Down comes the suitcase
> In go the clothes
> Bang slams the front door
> As another woman goes
> As another woman goes
> As another woman goes.
>
> *Chorus*
> Yes she still loves him
> And she still wants him
> No she cannot stay
> She's gotta get away
> It's a lonely town

When you've got no home
It's a question of
Be a slave in love
Or freedom on your own

Is she losing or is she winning
Is life ending or is it beginning (*End chorus.*)

Down streets of semis
Laid out in rows
Call from a 'phone box
To somebody she knows
To share her tale of woes
Before the money goes.

(*Chorus.*)

Stay on a friend's floor
Can't sleep all night
Wake in the morning
It isn't even light
Is what she's doing right
Life is such a fight

(*Chorus.*)

Is she losing or is she winning
Is life ending or is it beginning

Down comes the suitcase
In go the clothes
Bang slams the front door
As another woman goes
As another woman goes
As another woman goes
As another woman goes.

EVE's *house*

LINDA: I don't want to, Eve!

CELIA: No, come on, it'll take you out of yourself. It'll do you good!

LINDA: What is it?

MINA: It's a public meeting with NIREX. Mr NIREX is gonna be there. he's gonna tell us why we're being silly

LINDA: What's the point?

MARY: We'll go round the pub afterwards.

LINDA: It'll be boring.

EVE: No it won't, it will be fascinating. Especially compared to sitting in my front room listening to you go on about Melvyn all the time.

LINDA: Do I go on about him all the time?

ALL: Yep.

LINDA: Would you like me to find somewhere else to stay?

EVE: No, Lin, I just want you to do yourself a favour. Take an hour off from you and your old man and come and worry about the little things in life.

Bradstow Village Hall

MINA: When the government first announced its intention to find somewhere to dump nuclear waste in this country, not only did it propose to dump low-level waste, it also proposed to dump intermediate-level waste. It assured us this was perfectly safe. Then Chernobyl happened. And it dropped its plans to bury intermediate-level waste. Presumably because in the aftermath of the Russian disaster even this government found its casual approach to all things nuclear hard to swallow. In other words its original plan wasn't perfectly safe. Now that the dust has settled – excuse the pun – once again we are being told that the new plan to dump only low-level waste is perfectly safe. Give me one good reason why on earth we should accept that this assurance of perfect safety is any more reliable than the first?!

NIREX: The point is both assurances are quite correct.

MINA: Then why did the government change its mind?

NIREX: There are no scientific grounds for restricting the waste that might be disposed of in shallow burial grounds.

MARY: Burial grounds! We're gonna be a cemetery now are we?!

NIREX: But this is an area where it has proved particularly difficult to bridge the gap between scientists' assessment of risks and the honestly-held perceptions of the local communities.

MINA: If you want to bridge the credibility gap, stop lying!

NIREX: So the government accepted the distinction drawn by many between low-level and intermediate waste and recognised that many people would be reassured if the restriction was made. But there is no scientific need for it. It was essentially a humanitarian decision.

EVE: Leave it out! She doesn't know the meaning of the word!

NIREX: Can I just say, a great deal of low-level radioactive waste comes from hospitals and industry. We're talking about rubber gloves, syringes, paper towels, that sort of thing. We want to dispose of these articles in concrete trenches, twenty metres below the surface. We want to cover those trenches with two layers of concrete, one metre thick, and clay. We really are talking about a low-level containment exercise, believe me.

LINDA: You see, you're trying to make it sound like it's harmless. But if you've gotta keep it underground for three hundred years, I don't care if it's a picture of George Michael it must be bloody lethal!

NIREX: Modern concrete technology can easily contain it for that length of time.

LINDA: Is that what they used to build M25? It cracked up in a week!

NIREX: The nuclear programme in the UK has been operating since 1956 without a single radiation accident injuring a member of the public.

LINDA: Kids round power stations get leukaemia.

NIREX: You can receive more radiation holidaying in the granite areas of Cornwall or Scotland.

LINDA: Where do you live? I'll have your house. You have mine!

NIREX: It wouldn't worry me in the slightest to live in Bradstow . . . What do you say to that?

LINDA: I say you're here tonight doing your job. For you this is just a public relations exercise. I'm serious. I'm pregnant and I want to get out. Would you swop houses with me, please . . .? You're playing with the lives of all these people. And you're here tonight playing still, you bastard!

MARY's *favourite pub*

EVE: Girls, let us raise our glasses, both alcoholic and non-alcoholic, to someone who surprised us all tonight. We all of us know, the quiet ones are the ones you have to watch. But did any of us realise that the ones that won't say boo to a goose are even deadlier! She got him by the short and curlies. She swung him round her head. She dropped him down the toilet. And when she'd sorted out her husband she did the same to the man from NIREX. But seriously though, how can we lose; it was a joy to behold. Linda, we love you!

I've had enough

Tell you a little story
About a woman who travelled down South
Quiet little lady
Didn't like to open her mouth
Well one fine day
She got tough
She said Man
I've had enough.

Chorus

I have had enough
Lord, oh Lord
I've had enough
Well this woman gets going
When the going gets tough
I've had enough. (*End chorus.*)

She came to stay with Evie
She kipped down on her floor
That man don't change his mind
He'll never see me no more
I can mend a fuse
Fix a shelf
Have that baby
By myself.

(*Chorus.*)

She went to a meeting
With the NIREX company
Listen to the man
Spout a load of old baloney

You want the truth
Right in your lap
What you say
Is really total crap.
(*Chorus.*)

The meeting erupted
The Bradstow cats went wild
Who's that crazy woman
Got the boss man really riled.

Hell she's angry
Hell she's mad
Goes by the name
Of Linda Bragg.
(*Chorus.*)

Listen all you people
From the North down to the South
Don't take it lying down
Stand up and open your mouth.

Today's the day
We get tough
Listen man
We've had enough.
(*Chorus.*)

The GP's surgery

GP: What can I do for you, Mr Bragg?

MELVYN: It's about my wife, doctor.

GP: I thought it might be.

MELVYN: She's pregnant.

GP: Yes. I think I knew before you did.

MELVYN: I suppose so . . . She wants to have the baby at . . . not in hospital.

GP: That's right.

MELVYN: Well, I'm not keen.

GP: Good man.

MELVYN: Yes, well that's all very well but she's bloody gone.

She's gone . . . She's just gone.

GP: Has she ever done this sort of thing before?

MELVYN: No. She stayed with a friend for a bit. Now she's got a room in Bradstow. I'm going out of my mind. I can't sleep.

GP: Yes, well, I think what we'll do . . . is put you on a course of mild tranquilisers and see you in a month.

MELVYN: I'm not talking about me, I'm talking about her! I don't want a child of mine born in a bedsit!

GP: It's strange. She seems to have cut herself off from the help and protection of her husband and the medical profession for some reason.

MELVYN: I want you to do something about it.

GP: Absolutely, Mr Bragg . . . I think the only way we're going to get her back is to take her on for a home confinement.

MELVYN: Yes, but I don't want her to have a home confinement.

GP: Neither do I, Mr Bragg.

MELVYN: You can't give in to her. She's got to see sense.

GP: Leave it with me! Nice to see you! Don't worry! We'll get her back. If she trusts us we might be able to persuade her.

LINDA's *bedsit.*

MIDWIFE: Well it's a small room, but it's got everything. So it's fine as far as I'm concerned.

LINDA: I called you a childless bloody spinster.

MIDWIFE. You did.

LINDA: I'm ever so sorry.

MIDWIFE: Don't be. It's perfectly true. But there's enough of us having babies in the world without me feeling I'm letting the side down. We all have our part to play in keeping the whole shebang going, don't we?

LINDA: Why did the doctor change his mind?

MIDWIFE: He's very much against home births, normally. I haven't got a clue. To be honest with you, I'm not keen myself, especially the first. The thing is, if there are no complications, you can have it in a field! Imagine how it would have been the first million years every time a woman was pregnant, they said, hang on, we haven't invented hospitals yet.

LINDA: I suppose women died that was the only thing.

MIDWIFE: Oh yes, they did that right enough. But today we've got the telephone and the flying squad so I wouldn't bother with a will. Just get what's on the list. Two bowls, one bucket, a bed pan, a plastic sheet for the mattress, a jug of sterile water, a nailbrush, and a load of old newspaper.

LINDA: What are they for?

MIDWIFE: You put them round the bed. For the blood.

LINDA: Oh my god, what have I let myself in for?

MIDWIFE: You can always change your mind.

LINDA: No, I've decided.

MIDWIFE: That's what I wanted to hear.
Now, one other thing, Linda. My name's Valerie. And from now on we're in this together, right?

LINDA: Right.

MIDWIFE: Right.
LINDA *tries to hide a terrible pain in her abdomen.*
What's the matter? Where's the pain?

LINDA: In my stomach.

MIDWIFE: Is it like a period pain?

LINDA: Yes.

MIDWIFE: Have you had it before?

LINDA: It started just before you came.

MIDWIFE: Are you bleeding?

LINDA: A bit.

MIDWIFE: Get into bed and we'll decide what to do.

Night time in a labour ward. Someone moans.

WOMAN: What they got you in for?

LINDA: Bed rest.

WOMAN: Miscarriage?

LINDA: Threatened. I'll be all right if I'm careful.

WOMAN: We'd all be all right if we were careful.

A moan.

LINDA: Is that . . . someone in labour?

WOMAN: What?

A moan.

LINDA: That noise.

WOMAN: Oh that! Yes! I don't notice it anymore. Is this your
first?

LINDA: Yeah.

A moan.

WOMAN: I've got eight.

Labour Ward 109

You can hear us moaning
In the dead of night
We should be fast asleep
We should be tucked up tight
Like the snoozing night nurse
Underneath her light
Do we have one hell of a time

Chorus

We're the women in Maternity
The girls of labour ward 109.

We checked in nice and early
With the baby's pa
They shaved our pubic hair
Before he'd parked the car
Then they caught us napping
With the enema
Do we have one hell of a time
Find yourself the two girls
With the loudest scream
You can bet the bed you get
Is in between
I hate to think what's going on
Behind that screen

(Chorus.)

We love it, an even though we're not sick
We wouldn't miss it, you'll always find us here

> You want to join us, just find a fella and click
> You can come back almost each and every single year
> Some of us are waiting
> For our waters to break
> Some of us have had ours
> And we think we're great
> And one's spent sixteen hours
> Trying to dilate
> Do we have one hell of a time
>
> Even when you've given birth
> You're still not done
> Soon your boobs are like balloons
> And weigh two ton
> And every doctor checks
> The stitches in your bum.
>
> (*Chorus*.)

MELVYN: Hello Linda!

LINDA: Melvyn!

MELVYN: How are you?

LINDA: I'm fine. We're both fine.

MELVYN: I bought you some bananas. For the folic acid. I've been reading your pregnancy book. You left it behind.

LINDA: Funny, I keep fancying bananas.

MELVYN: It helps your body absorb iron. To make all the extra blood.

LINDA: Are you a doctor?

MELVYN: No, I never really bothered.

LINDA: Have I been very silly, Melvyn?

MELVYN: No, I think you've just been what you are deep down. A very determined woman.

LINDA: D'you think so?

MELVYN: I've often told you that. I've often said to you, Linda, you're bloody impossible, woman!

LINDA: It's not quite so straightforward as I thought this having a baby business. You don't realise, there's one way for it to go right. And a hundred other ways it can go wrong. I mean it's a little life. You can't take chances.

MELVYN: Come home, love.

LINDA: Where will I have the baby?

MELVYN: Where you and I decide it's best. Together.

LINDA: You know the doctor's taken me on for a home birth, don't you.

MELVYN: Has he? Well, I'm sure he knows what he's doing.

LINDA: Is there a chance you could change your mind?

MELVYN: I would have thought so. As long as there's a chance you could change yours.

LINDA: All right, it's a deal!

MELVYN: When are you coming out?

LINDA: No-one's said. I'm bored out me mind.

MELVYN: Well find out and ring me and I'll get the place cleaned up and buy some food.

LINDA: What you been eating?

MELVYN: I don't know, rubbish! Tins! Chips! Take-aways, mostly.

LINDA: How's work?

MELVYN: It's going very well.

LINDA: Good.

MELVYN: We've got the contract to do the electrics on the site.

LINDA: What site?

MELVYN: They're gonna have quite a little engineering village there while they do the survey.

LINDA: What site?

MELVYN: What you looking at me like that for?

LINDA: You're working for NIREX?

MELVYN: No, I'm not, I'm working for the firm.

LINDA: What's the difference?! The firm's working for NIREX!

MELVYN: All the difference in the world. I can't tell the firm what to do, can I? I can't say, don't sign that contract, my wife doesn't approve.

LINDA: I don't believe it. I'm scared stiff and you're going to help them build the bloody thing. You're risking our baby's life, that's what you're doing!

MELVYN: No, Linda, I'm just trying to scrape a bit of a future together. you're the one who's in hospital risking lives!

EVE: Linda, lovey! How you doing? You look great! Who bought you all these bananas?

CELIA: I'm sorry, darling, we've had to come all together. It was the only time we could make.

MARY: Can you drink in here? I've bought you a few bottles of medicinal Guinness.

MINA: Linda, NIREX is going to try and get onto the site tomorrow morning. We're going to mount a 24-hour blockade. This is 100% organic honey, by the way, you'll love it!

MARY: Have you got a bottle opener? Doesn't matter, I can do it with my teeth.

EVE: We reckon there's gonna be at least a thousand people there!

MINA: Going on reactions, the whole village is going to turn out.

CELIA: Linda, even I'm going. I've got a crash helmet and a dustbin lid! I can't wait!

LINDA: Right. Put a pillow in me bed and draw the curtains.

EVE: You're meant to be resting.

LINDA: No, I've done all that! I'm striking a blow for freedom. Come on!

I've Had Enough (*Reprise*)

Tell you a little story
About a woman who travelled down South
Quiet little lady
Didn't like to open her mouth
Well one find day
She got tough
She said Man
I've had enough.
I have had enough
Lord, oh Lord
I've had enough
Well this woman gets going
When the going gets tough
I've had enough.

PART TWO

The women enter.

MARY: Would you say we've changed?

MINA: Yes, I've changed.

LINDA: I would say I've changed.

CELIA: I have definitely changed. God, how I've changed!

EVE: Yeah, I've changed. A lot.

MARY: How would you say we have changed?

MINA: As a person I feel bigger.

LINDA: With everything, we've grown.

CELIA: I'm twice the person I was.

EVE: There's more to us now, somehow.

CELIA: And d'you know what did it? When those coppers pinned us to the ground at four o'clock in the morning and stopped us sounding the alarm. The seeds of change were sown. One hundred policemen to break a blockade manned by five pregnant women! I still find the whole thing completely un-English. They hadn't got the guts to come during the first week when the village was there in strength. They hadn't even got the guts to come when the men were doing a stint. I didn't vote for Margaret Thatcher to be treated like a coal miner!

I've Changed

Chorus

I've changed
We've all changed
I'm a very different woman
I've changed
We've all changed
And let me tell you how
I've changed
We've all changed
Got a very altered outlook
I'm wise
I'm really wised-up now.
I guess a lot of people

Have known it all along
You don't have to break the law
To find you're in the wrong
It's just a different vision
From the powers that be
And soon its gone
Pretty soon it's missing
What's it called
Democracy
I guess a lot of people
Have known it all the time
But I really thought this country
Could hear a voice like mine
Now I've started looking
And it's plain to see
Who runs the show
Someone's got it sewn-up
And it isn't you and me
(*Chorus.*)

MARY: No, I mean, would you say we were fatter?

EVE: Fatter?! Oh, yeah, we're fatter.

MARY: We're bound to be, aren't we?

EVE: Yes.

MARY: I've just seen the programme Three months go past in the interval.

EVE: That's right.

MARY: That's why we put the padding on.

EVE: Mary! . . . you're not helping the illusion, are you?

MARY: Sorry.

MINA: Okay, can we sort out what we're going to do. Celia can you explain your plan.

CELIA: Okay, my little scheme is to go round all the portacabins on the site and bung up the locks with superglue. I've had a word with Jack about it.

MINA: Jack?

CELIA: He's my local bobby. He's pretty much one of us. And he's given me a tip. Leave one lock unstuck. Otherwise they can do you for incarceration. And that's a serious offence.

MINA: Okay, that's one idea . . .

EVE: What's in it for us?

CELIA: They can't get at their gear. We stop them working for a day.

EVE: Yeah, glue up overnight. Sounds great.

MINA: What about Security? The ex-football hooligans with walky-talkies.

CELIA: They seem to fall asleep round about two in the morning, poor loves.

MINA: Right, so what do people think?

MARY: Can we trust Jack?

CELIA: We don't have to trust Jack. He's just given us some advice.

MARY: It could be a trick.

CELIA: What are you talking about, Mary?

MARY: I don't know. It's what they say on the television . . . Did you know his wife was having a baby?

CELIA: Yes, she's just had a test for spina bifida.
A ripple of fear runs round the group.
She's okay.

EVE: I couldn't cope with having a baby that was handicapped, could you?

MINA: I think you just have to, don't you?

EVE: I'm not sure I can cope with having an ordinary one . . . I'm not sure I can cope with just having it. Full stop. You know what having a baby is meant to be like, don't you?

CELIA: What?

EVE: Shitting a grapefruit.

CELIA: Well that's given us something to think about.

EVE: D'you know what the worst pain in the world is? Having your first baby. D'you know what the second worst pain is? Having your second baby. D'you know what comes third? Being tortured.

CELIA: Thank you very very much, Eve. That's really helped my little pile of confidence that I've been scraping together over the last few months.

MARY: During the interval.

EVE: It's a fact!

MARY: Yes, but it's only one way of seeing things, Eve.

MINA: That's right. I was talking to a friend of mine the other night. She's got a couple of kids. We were having some camomile tea. I think. It may have been rosehip. Anyway, she said people always go on about the pain of childbirth, but with hers she said she tried to experience the event as an emotional rather than physical thing. In other words, instead of being overtaken by all those film images of the agonised woman in labour, she concentrated on the idea of herself as an unfolding flower more.

CELIA: And did it make a difference?

MINA: No. She said it still felt like taking hold of your top lip and stretching it over your head.

LINDA: The thing about glueing up the locks is it won't get us any publicity. What we should do is tell the papers and chain ourselves to the drilling rig.

LINDA, EVE *and* CELIA *are chained to a drilling rig.* LEN, *the Project Manager, approaches.*

LEN: All right, ladies. You've made your point. Who's got the key?

LINDA: We didn't bring it with us, I'm afraid.

EVE: You don't need a key to lock a padlock, do you?

CELIA: We couldn't go. Even if we wanted to. Sorry!

LEN: Haven't you got anything better to do with your time than waste mine and my men's?

LINDA: Oh dear, we're wasting *men's* time girls! Did you know? A second of men's time is worth an hour of women's.

LEN: What have we got here then? A little lesbian, is it?

LINDA: Yes, that's it! We're all pregnant lesbians!

LEN: It did strike me you were all on the plump side. But a gentleman doesn't make personal remarks about a woman's figure, does he?

CELIA: How would you know what a gentleman did?

LEN: Frankly, I find it a sad reflection of our times that you are prepared to do this to the beautiful condition of expectant motherhood. It's not just you chained to that rig. Three little innocent children are chained to that rig with you. Assuming, of course, no multiple pregnancies. Oh yes, I know all the medical terms. I may be a mere male in your eyes, but I have paced up and down outside the delivery room on a number of occasions. I thought using sport for political ends was bad enough. But when the unborn foetus is press-ganged into service by its own mother, then I despair for mankind's very existence.

EVE: So, it's you who writes them, is it?!

LEN: Sorry?

EVE: Margaret Thatcher's speeches! You sanctimonius little wanker!

LEN: Is this the mouth of a mother?

EVE: Too bloody right it is!

LEN *switches on his walky-talky.*

LEN: Big Boy to Little John! Big Boy to Little John! . . . Little John? . . . Big Boy speaking . . . Big Boy! . . . Len! . . . Fine! . . . How are you? . . . good! Listen, I've got three NAP's on site unable to vacate due to malicious attachment to company property . . . What d'you mean, you don't know what I'm talking about?! . . . I've got three pregnant women chained to the drilling rig! . . . The blokes can't start. They've been waiting all morning! . . . Request assistance of maintenance crew . . . Well send someone up with the wire cutters then you pillock! (*To* LINDA, EVE and CELIA.) You do realise you could go to prison for this don't you? There's an injunction against anyone in the village interfering.

CELIA: You do realise that you're a big wimp, don't you, Big Boy!

LEN: What sort of men have wives like you? I suppose they have beards and go jogging and drink dry white wine, don't they. We didn't get a lot of those in the Falklands, thank God. What would that sort do if they came face to face with an Exocet missile, eh?

LINDA: Die?

LEN: They would go completely to pieces. I didn't. Goose
Green. Stanley. Bomb Alley. There were times I came that
close to – I was inches away from – His Royal Highness,
Prince Andrew. Weight for weight I've got more metal in my
head than brain. But I refuse to see myself as a cripple. I can
float head down; I've taken up water ballet; I'm fighting back
without the help of a television documentary. Is this what I did
it all for? So that men like your husbands can let wives like
you behave like this! God, it makes me sick!
MELVYN *arrives.*

MELVYN: I've brought the wire cutters, Len.

LEN: Melvyn, do you recognise any of these?!

MELVYN: How d'you mean?

LEN: You're a local lad. Are you familiar with any of them?
'Cos we'll want to get the names right on the writ, won't we?
MELVYN *stares hard in disbelief.*
Take your time. There's no hurry. They're not going anywhere
just yet.
MELVYN *is speechless.*
What would you say to a wife of yours if she was standing in
the way of progress like this, Melvyn?

LINDA: Yes, what would you say, Melvyn?

MELVYN: What d'you want me to do, Len? Just cut 'em free?

LINDA: No, he wants you to say, love!

LEN: You'd be like me, Melvyn, I know! You wouldn't stand for
it. You'd say, 'Woman, do as you're told!' And that would be
enough. Am I right, Melvyn?

LINDA: Is he right, Melvyn?

MELVYN: Well, I don't know if they would be the exact
words . . .

LEN: But something along those lines. Absolutely! You may be
able to wrap your husbands round your little fingers, ladies,
but my lads are made of sterner stuff. They've got lead in their
pencils! Now, who are they, Melvyn?

MELVYN: I don't know, Len. I've not actually lived here very
long, yet, I'm sorry.

LEN: Never mind, my son you've tried, that's all that matters.

We'll just have to look in the local paper, won't we? They've taken enough photos this morning, haven't they ladies? All right, Melvyn, cut 'em loose, let 'em go! For the moment.

The waiting room at the ante-natal clinic.

MIDWIFE: Good morning, ladies!

ALL: Good morning Valerie!

MIDWIFE: You all look wonderful! Full of the joys of motherhood!

EVE: Full of the joys of what?!

MIDWIFE: Are you complaining again, Eve?

EVE: Yep.

MIDWIFE: What's wrong now?

EVE: We think nine months is too long.

MIDWIFE: How long would you prefer?

EVE: About a week.

MIDWIFE: Would you like to tell me why?

Move Over Momma

Once I had a body
It was mine all mine
Did what I told it
Most of the time.

Then my baby moved in
Made himself at home
Nowadays my body ain't my own.

Chorus

Move over Momma
I need some elbow room.
Move over Momma
Need some space inside this womb

Move over Momma
You're gonna have to choose
If you wanna baby
Got to pay your baby dues (*End Chorus.*)

Talking 'bout your diet
Think it only best
I'll eat all the good stuff

You can have the rest
Make no bones without it
I'm a low-down thief
If you don't score me calcium
I'll take all your teeth
(*Chorus*.)

This thing is getting bigger
Bigger every way
Can't wait until you say
You're moving out today.

Momma listen to me
Moaning makes me yawn
You think you've got your troubles
Wait till I've been born.

(*Chorus*.)

Take me to the clinic
Doc will see you now
Tell him how you're feeling
Like a pregnant cow.

Climb up on the scales
And roll up both your sleeves
Undress behind the curtain
Lie on the couch
Open wide
Take a deep breath
Say aah
Smile
And pass a urine sample please.

(*Chorus*.)

MIDWIFE: Well, I sympathise, ladies, but nothing is free in this
life. And as far as having a baby goes the manufacturer's
recommended retail price is forty weeks. Take it or leave it.
Now, who are we meant to be seeing first? Come along,
Linda, let's have a look at you.
MIDWIFE *takes* LINDA's *blood pressure*.
Well, how does it feel to be a personality with your photograph
in the local paper? I must say I wouldn't have known it was
you without the name underneath. But it's not every day one

of my ladies gets into the paper for attaching herself to a piece
of engineering apparatus. You never know, if you're going to
make a habit of it you might get yourself sponsored by a firm
selling maternity dresses. God love us, did you run here,
Linda?! You're one hundred and thirty five over ninety!

LINDA: Is that high?

MIDWIFE: Not for a four minute mile, no. Show me your
ankles.

LINDA *does*.

How d'you feel?

LINDA: Terrible . . . I've just been served with a writ.

MIDWIFE: A writ?! Whatever for?

LINDA: I've got to appear at the High Court next Tuesday . . .
to show why I should not be gaoled for allegedly intimidating
and menacing NIREX workers . . . I don't know how I've
meant to have done that. They're all great big six-foot blokes,
most of them!

MIDWIFE: Oh my God, Linda! What are you playing at?!
You're 29 weeks pregnant and you're behaving like a bloody
marine! It's got to stop! Go home and take it easy for a
change. Dig up the back garden or something.

LINDA's *house.*
Laughter.

LEN: Girls! Come in! Sit down! Take your coats off!

JACKIE: What we drinking to?

LEN: To us! Old friends!

JACKIE: Old friends! We've only known you an hour and a
half!

LEN: True, my love, but you must admit a lot of liquid has
flown under our bridge in that short space of time. We have
possibly experienced, you and me, more in those ninety
minutes than some men and women do in a whole lifetime. So
how about telling one another our names?

JACKIE: She's Gerry. I'm Jackie.

LEN: Jackie and Gerry! Fantastic! Je m'appelle, Leonard!

JACKIE: Oh frigging hell!

LEN: Len to me friends. Between the sheets or over the radio also known as Big Boy!

JACKIE: Sounds disgusting. Tell me more.

GERRY: What's his name then?

LEN: This is the man whose lounge we are sitting in. The man whose wife has very conveniently gone away for the weekend to look after her ill mother. This is my colleague from work. The mighty Melvyn!

GERRY: Melvyn?!

MELVYN: Yeah, Melvyn. What's wrong with that?

GERRY: It's wet, ain't it?!

MELVYN: No.

GERRY: You wouldn't get far in the charts with a name like that.

MELVYN: I'm an electrician.

GERRY: I'll call you Sparky.

MELVYN: No, call me Melvyn. You'd look silly with a fat lip! *Everyone laughs.*

LEN: Okay, now we all know one another. And are very obviously enjoying one another's company. Jackie, my love, would you care to . . . partake in a little vertical sex?

JACKIE: Sounds disgusting! Tell me more! *They dance.*

GERRY: Do you always bring strange women home when your wife's away, melvyn?

MELVYN: Well, when the pub's closed, and you haven't got a video, there's not a lot else, is there? Look, I'm sorry about me name. I'm sorry I'm not a pop star. All I'm doing is trying to keep in with me boss. He wants to get his leg over and he's got nowhere else to go. Okay?

GERRY: And you don't, I suppose.

MELVYN: No, I don't, thank you very much.

GERRY: I wasn't offering.

MELVYN: I'm very pleased to hear it.

GERRY: Let's go upstairs!

MELVYN: What for?

GERRY: I've changed me mind.

MELVYN: Don't muck about.

GERRY: I mean it.

MELVYN: Are you sure?

GERRY: Thought you weren't interested.

MELWYN: What you playing at?

GERRY: You got any more of that lager, Melvyn?

MELVYN: Have I got to get you drunk beforehand?

GERRY: Before what?

MELVYN: I'll look in the fridge.
He stands up and sees LINDA *has come in.*
What do you want?

LEN: Bloody hell! What's she doing here?! Now be fair, love, we're off duty. You can't barge into people's houses and chain yourself up when they're off duty!

LINDA: I live here! I'm his wife!

LEN: His wife?!

LINDA: That's right.

JACKIE: How's your mum?

LINDA: And who are these two specimens, Melvyn?

MELVYN: No one in particular, Linda.

GERRY: Just someone your husband picked up in a pub, Mrs Bragg.

MELVYN: Look, you walked out! I'm over 21! I can do what I like!

LINDA: I'm carrying your child and you're playing around with prostitutes!

GERRY: I beg your pardon!

LINDA: You heard!

GERRY: Yes, I did.
She slaps LINDA.
LINDA *takes it and slaps her back.*
And I didn't like it.

LINDA: That should have been for him, not you. I'm sorry.

Silence.
I came for me suit. I've got to go to court on Tuesday. If you want to know why, ask your boss.

Outside the high court in London. The ante-natal group contemplates the audience.

EVE: Look at them all!

MARY: Stuck up lot!

CELIA: More money than sense most of them.

MINA: Killing themselves with exhaust fumes.

EVE: I hate London!

MARY: He looks nice.

CELIA: Is that what you call fashion?

MINA: It's what he calls fashion.

EVE: Oh isn't it a shame!

MARY: I think he looks nice.

EVE: How you feeling, Lin?

LINDA: I've just spoken to my Counsel. They've changed it from half-past-ten to half-past-eleven.

CELIA: What for?

LINDA: They didn't give a reason.

EVE: What we gonna do?

MARY: The pubs are open . . . well, we can't stand about on the pavement all morning!

MINA: We could hand out some leaflets. Publicise our case.

EVE: What, to this lot?

MINA: Yes, why not?

MARY (*to the man in the audience*): Would you like a leaflet?

CELIA: Mary, you're a married woman!

MARY: Celia, I'm offering him a leaflet not my body.

The Leaflet Song

Please accept this leaflet
It's a terrifying read
It'll scare the shit right from you
Might never choose to breed.

Come on take me leaflet
It only says you'll die
Won't you face the nightmare
You mustn't be so shy.
(*Chorus.*)

Oh there's always some guy saying
Something nasty's going on
Someone somewhere's doing some such
The whole world's going wrong.

If you ever stopped and pondered
Everything that this guy said
You're just a simple fella
It would destroy your bleeding head. (*End chorus.*)

Well it's only human
When you see me in the street
To disregard a woman
Being somewhat indiscreet.

Maggie wouldn't do it
If it wasn't for the best
It's a democratic country
With an independent press.
(*Chorus.*)

So if I get heavy
While the chaps are getting pissed
Put me down as female
With me knickers in a twist.

Believe me I appreciate
You're just a little man
You'll never change the way things are
'Cos you don't think you can.
(*Chorus.*)

Please accept this leaflet
It's a terrifying read . . .
Song is interrupted by MINA.

MINA: Hold it, hold it, hold it! I'm not sure we're getting
through. I think we might be putting them off a bit. In fact I
think we're probably scaring them to death, actually. I think

we ought to try the nice version.

Please accept this leaflet.
It's an interesting read.
It's got serious implications
Perhaps we ought to heed.

Come on take my leaflet.
You personally won't die
It's someone else's nightmare
You might quite like to try.

ALL: No!
They revert to the 'nasty' version and belt out a final chorus.

EVE: Linda, come on! It's time to go in! Come on, we're gonna be late!

LINDA: Say no to nuclear dumping!

MELVYN: Thank you very much . . .
Suddenly she recognises him.

LINDA: What are you doing here, Melvyn?

MELVYN: Well, you know what I'm like. Just popped up to London . . . to find myself a woman . . . Hello!

LINDA: Shouldn't you be at work?

MELVYN: Yeah.

EVE: Linda!

LINDA: I've got to go.

MELVYN: I thought you might need some support.

EVE: Linda!

LINDA: I've got some support!

MELVYN: Don't be like that . . . What court are you in?

LINDA: Number twelve.

Court room 12

COUNSEL AGAINST: The Court will rise . . . All right, if that's the way you're going to behave, 2B, you can all sit down again. No one will leave this room until I say so. I'm not interested in your complaints. Be quiet! . . . My Lord, Linda Bragg, I submit, wilfully obstructed a servant of the Crown as he attempted to go about the duty laid down for him by Act of

Parliament. In the clear knowledge that to do so was in open defiance of a ruling authorised by your Lordship . . . When I give out sixteen protractors I expect to get back sixteen protractors! Not fifteen protractors! Take the bags off the top of your desks! No one is going home until my cigar box has its full compliment of sixteen protractors. Where d'you think you're going Linda Bragg?

LINDA: Please, sir, it's me birthday, I've got to go, I'm having a party, sir, me cousin's coming, she's going to Australia tomorrow, I'll never see her again, sir, I've got to go, sir!

COUNSEL AGAINST: I don't care if your entire family is in chains and bound for Botany Bay, I've told you to sit down.

MELVYN: Please sir, her cousin's emigrating, you've got to let her go, sir.

COUNSEL AGAINST: No one's asking you, Melvyn, shut up! . . . I said sit down! . . . sit down! . . . Are you going to sit down?!

LINDA: No.

COUNSEL AGAINST: I beg your pardon!

LINDA: No.

COUNSEL AGAINST: No, what?!

LINDA: No, I'm not.

COUNSEL AGAINST: Don't push your luck, little girl! No, what?!

LINDA: No, I'm not . . . you bastard.

COUNSEL AGAINST: In the circumstances, My Lord, I respectfully suggest, there is no reason why she should not be subject to the full force of the law.

JUDGE: Can we just get one thing straight?

COUNSEL AGAINST: My Lord, yes, by all means.

JUDGE: You're not saying she took the protractor, are you?

COUNSEL AGAINST: My Lord, no.

JUDGE: Because that would be a very serious matter.

COUNSEL AGAINST: My Lord, yes. My Lord, respectfully, the point I'm trying to make . . .

JUDGE: I think I've got the point, thank you. You've made

your point most clearly, thank you very much . . . I think I should hear what Mrs Bragg's Counsel has to say.

COUNSEL FOR: I don't deny for one minute what she did was wrong, headmaster. All I'm saying is she's only a child and it was her birthday.

COUNSEL AGAINST: My Lord, it was a considered, insolent act of disobedience.

COUNSEL FOR: I've always brought her up to show respect where respect is due. I've told her time after time, if they respect you, you respect them.

COUNSEL AGAINST: My Lord, she broke your ruling deliberately. She showed no respect for your authority whatsoever.

COUNSEL FOR: I know she called him a bastard. And that's not very nice. But what would you call someone who stopped a little kiddie going to her own birthday party?

JUDGE: Yes, it's not a disproportionate response in the circumstances. He is a bit of a bastard, there's no getting away from it. Aren't you?

COUNSEL AGAINST: My Lord, without doubt, I am, yes.

JUDGE: Mrs Bragg is pregnant, I believe.

COUNSEL FOR: She is married, Headmaster.

JUDGE: Good, I'm pleased to hear it. Well now, I can't allow my rulings to be broken. That's quite obvious. On the other hand, Mrs Bragg's Counsel has very wisely not argued that Mrs Bragg didn't breach a previous judgement of mine. She has instead suggested that Mrs Bragg acted in the heat of the moment. And I'm inclined to accept this. I can't honestly see how Mrs Bragg's detention would help the situation. Mrs Bragg I'm sure has suffered enough in the last few days. Costs, of course, are a different matter. She will, I think, have to bear those. I would point out that were I to be presented with a similar set of circumstances again, I imagine this is not a judgement I would be likely to arrive at a second time.

COUNSEL AGAINST: The Court will rise.

The JUDGE *stands, nods and disappears.*

In the entrance hall of the high court.

CELIA: That judge, believe me, was a sweetie!

LINDA: I didn't understand a word of it. I mean I broke the law, didn't I?

CELIA: You did. I would have thrown the book at you, darling.

EVE: They didn't want you, Lin! They don't want a martyr, that's what it is.

MARY: You see they won't hang a woman when she's pregnant, that's the point, Linda.

CELIA: You didn't know you were facing the death penalty, did you?

EVE: Becoming a mother is more of a punishment!

MELVYN: Very well done!

LINDA: Thanks for coming, Melvyn.

MELVYN: How you getting back?

LINDA: We got a day return on the train. We muscled in on a poker school on the way up.

MELVYN: Do you want a lift?

LINDA: We're giving them a chance to get their money back on the way home.

MELVYN: I would just like us to talk, that's all.

LINDA: What about?

MELVYN: I've shifted me ground slightly.

LINDA: How d'you mean?

MELVYN: I think I should give up me job and you should have the baby at home.

LINDA: Suddenly everyone's agreeing with me!

MELVYN: Would you like to come round for a meal and talk about it?

LINDA: I don't believe this! Melvyn, you can't cook!

MELVYN: You've been gone a long time. I've learnt.

MELVYN: What? To cook?!

MELVYN: No, where you go in Sainsbury's for the frozen dinners.

LINDA: Okay.

MELVYN: Bring the baby. What does it eat?
LINDA: Same as me.
MELVYN: Friday night?
LINDA: Yeah.
MELVYN: Great! I'd better go. I'm on a meter.

Let's Take The Train Home

Let's take the train home
You and I
Get a cup of coffee
Watch the world go by.
The troubles we had today
Have packed up and flown away
There isn't a cloud
In the whole darn sky.

Let's take the train home
You and I.
Deal out those cards
My luck is riding high
Owe a lawyer five thousand pound
Should clear that with one more round

Let's take the train home
You and I
Because we've won we've won
We've won our case
We've won our case
Today
We've won our case
We've won our case
We've won our case
We've won
We've won our case
We've won our case
We've won hip hip
Hooray

Let's take the train home
You and I
If we're together sister
We'll get by

Lean on me that's okay
I'm right beside you all the way
The troubles we had today
Have packed up and flown away
We're tying one on tonight
That man of mine's seen the light
So let's take the train home
Let's take the train home
You and I.

LINDA's *house.*

LINDA: That was lovely, Melvyn. I haven't eaten so . . . much for a long time.

MELVYN: We're not half way through yet, love! We've still got the coffee, cheese and biscuits, fruit, brandy, port, liquers and 'after-eights' yet!

LINDA: Oh, no! I couldn't eat another thing!

MELVYN: You're joking, we've hardly started!

LINDA: Melvyn, I've had enough, thank you very much.

MELVYN: Don't be daft! You're eating for two, aren't you?

LINDA: This is what I've been trying to say to you all evening. If I come back you've got to let me be.

MELVYN: I just wanted you to try me fresh fruit salad. I made it myself. From fresh fruit . . . It doesn't matter. I'll take it to work in me sandwiches.

LINDA: You know I love you, don't you?

MELVYN: No.

LINDA: I wouldn't be here otherwise.

MELVYN: So why won't you come back?

LINDA: I've told you. I can't. Not while you're doing what you're doing . . .

MELVYN: I'll look for something else.

LINDA: I know it's not easy. I know you've got to earn money.

MELVYN: You never know it might take care of itself. It'll all be over in four months. Len told me.

LINDA: You're finishing in four months?

MELVYN: Yeah, the survey's nearly done. Don't broadcast it! No-one's meant to know.

LINDA: Melvyn, hang on! I can't keep something like that to myself. It's important.

MELVYN: Okay, just don't say I told you, that's all.

LINDA: No, all right, fair enough.

MELVYN: Why is it important?

LINDA: Well . . . for one thing, if there's four months, I'll be able to concentrate on having the baby instead of going down the site every day. I only have to think about that place nowadays and I'm exhausted.

MELVYN: I can't believe it. Someone's in there.
He puts his hand on LINDA's *bulge and snatches it away.*

LINDA: What's the matter?

MELVYN: I felt something move! My baby shook my hand!

LINDA: You're lucky! Your baby usually kicks me in the ribs!

The ante-natal group is attending their last ante-natal class.

MIDWIFE: In a very uncertain world, ladies, I can guarantee you one thing. This time next month, you won't be pregnant.

EVE: Well, thank Christ for that!

MIDWIFE: And believe it or not, these nine months – when you feel like you've been pregnant all your life – will suddenly seem like the dim and distant past and you'll hardly remember a thing about them. Until you do it all over again of course.

EVE: You must be joking.

MIDWIFE: And you know who'll be the first to repeat it, don't you, Eve; I'll put money on it!

EVE: No way, Val! After this we're having twin beds.

MIDWIFE: We don't recommend it as one of the more reliable methods of contraception, Eve.

EVE: 100% safe, darling! My old man won't walk anywhere!

MIDWIFE: Well, we'll see. Now are there any questions about any of the subjects we've dealt with over the last few weeks? Anything about labour? Or breast feeding? Anything you're not sure of? Or you're worried about? Anything about relaxing or how to breathe? I don't mind what we talk about . . . As long as it's not the dump.

MARY: Valerie!

MIDWIFE: Mary.

MARY: How soon after having the baby can we . . . is it safe to . . .

MIDWIFE: Make love?

MARY: Drink alcohol.

MIDWIFE: Well, Mary, if I deliver your baby, as soon as you like. If someone else delivers it, don't start till I get there! Seriously, though, it will affect your milk. So moderation in all things!

MINA: Valerie, what about husbands?

MIDWIFE: That's a very large topic, Mina!

MINA: No being present.

MIDWIFE: Haven't you spoken to the hospital about that, yet?

MINA: Well, yes, I have actually. But what about having more than one?

MIDWIFE: Husband?

MINA: No, people present.

MIDWIFE: Who did you have in mind?

MINA: My yoga teacher.

MIDWIFE: They might let you have two. On the other hand you might have to choose.

MINA: You see, I think Stan will be great playing the guitar and taking the photos. But Naomi will be far better with the breathing and the birthing stool.

MIDWIFE: You'll just have to ask them . . . What about you, Linda? Any little worries we can clear up?

LINDA: Don't think so, Valerie, thank you very much.

MIDWIFE: Nothing bothering you at all?

LINDA: Can't think of anything . . . Except everything.

MIDWIFE: You're not worried about the possibility of having a snip and a stitch and then having a bowel movement afterwards or anything like that?

LINDA: Well I *wasn't* worried about that. Now you mention it I realise I'm petrified.

MIDWIFE: I'll give you a tip. Don't be!

LINDA: Thanks, Val!

MIDWIFE: Is there anything else at all? . . . No, well I'm sure you'll all do fine!

EVE: Roll on the day! I can hardly wait . . . Can you imagine it?

Today's The Day

Oh – I gotta
Low back pain
It's sort of – oh
Here it comes again.

Tell you honey
Ain't no doubt
What goes in
Must come right on out.

Pack my case
Is the car okay
'Phone the nurse
'Cos today's the day.

Chorus

Today's the day I've waited for
A day not like any other
I'm starry-eyed, I'm petrified
I'm going to be a mother. (*End chorus.*)

Eve loved Adam
On Day One
Nine months later
She had a son.

Who needs an apple
Who needs a snake
We're all still making
The same mistake.

Pack my case
Is the car okay

'Phone the nurse
Today's the day.

Today's the day I've waited for
A day not like any other
I'm starry-eyed – I'm petrified
I'm gonna be a mother.

Oh – I gotta
Low back pain
It's sort of – oh
Here it comes again.

Tell you honey
Ain't no doubt
What goes in
Must come right on out.

Pack my case
Is the car okay
'Phone the nurse
Today's the day.

(*Chorus..*)

The ante-natal group is outside the gate to the NIREX *enclosure on the airfield. It's early morning. The contractors haven't yet arrived for work.*

CELIA: What are we doing here at this hour of the morning?

MINA: Taking our turn.

CELIA: I thought the idea was we could ease up a bit now we know the finishing date.

EVE: We have eased up, Celia.

CELIA: Have we? Oh good!

MARY: I've never really seen the point of this. We don't stop them working, do we?

LINDA: No.

MARY: We just have a bit of a chat.

CELIA: Mary, we don't chat! You chat.

MARY: Well, it seems so juvenile not talking.

MINA: What is there to say to men like that? They are the enemy.

MARY: Melvyn's not the enemy. He spilled the beans.

MINA: He is different.

MARY: They might all be different. Given the chance. If someone spoke pleasantly to them.

EVE: Who are you? The Fairy Godmother?!
They wait on a moment.

MARY: So what is the point of being here when they arrive, then?
They wait on a bit more.

EVE: Well, someone tell her for God's sake!

MINA: Well . . . Linda, do you want to tell her?

LINDA: What?

MINA: Why we're here.

LINDA: My back is killing me.

MINA: You're not going into labour, are you?

LINDA: I shouldn't think so.

MINA: Why not?

LINDA: Because I'm meant to have it today. You never have it on the day you're meant to . . . Oh, that's better! It's gone a bit.

MARY: Len's just got out of his car.

MINA: We are demonstrating a presence, Mary. That's one of the reasons we're here . . . To show them we're here.

LEN: Good morning, Ladies! And how's my favourite group of urban guerillas this morning? . . . Looking forward to the weekend? Smashing! . . . Yes! Well, I mustn't keep you, I daresay you've got a very busy morning ahead of you! Nice of you to stop and talk! 'Bye for now!

LINDA: We reported you for working over the deadline on Tuesday, you know that, don't you. By law you're meant to stop at seven. You went on to half-past-eight.

LEN: Don't give me that Linda! When have you ever been bothered about the law?

LINDA: I recognise the law!

LEN: When it suits you. you were found guilty of breaking an injunction. You'd be inside now if you weren't pregnant.

A contraction overtakes LINDA. *She sits down.*
   Don't start sitting down, young lady!
EVE: I'd still be here, though, Len!
LEN: Well, aren't I the lucky one, Eve . . .
EVE: Why don't you piss down your leg and play with the
   steam.
LEN: . . . Because you are one of the few real ladies left.
   Haven't seen so much of you recently. Haven't seen so much
   of anyone recently, come to that. Bradstow hasn't decided
   we're not such a bad thing after all, has it?
MINA: Don't worry, we'll give you a decent send off before you
   go!
LEN: I doubt it.
MINA: Why?
LEN (*aside*): I wonder if I should tell them, ladies and
   gentlemen . . . yes, why not. (*To the women..*) Because,
   ladies, we are going today.
LINDA: You've got another two months!
LEN: Have we? . . . who told you that?
LINDA: You're not due to finish for another two months.
LEN: I leaked a false finishing date via Melvyn the unsuspecting
   mole. We're done. And you've let us off lightly. Ever been
   had, ladies? . . . Silly question, you must have been!
LINDA: You bastard!
LEN: We'll be coming out with the lorry in a minute, girls. Do
   mind your backs.
   LEN *goes through the gate.* LINDA *has a contraction.*
LINDA: Eve, this has got to be it! It's killing me!
EVE: Oh my God, Lin, I can't remember what to do! My mind's
   gone blank.
MINA: Go and get your car, Celia!
CELIA: Right!
LINDA: Celia!
CELIA: What Linda?
LINDA: It's all right, don't bother, I'm not going anywhere!

CELIA: What you talking about.

LINDA: Just phone Valerie. Ask her to come please. Tell her I'm having contractions about every ten minutes. And would she come please. Here.

EVE: Linda, you can't have it here!

LINDA: I'm having it just there. And that man gets nothing out those gates today! I swear it! Bastard! I want Melvyn. Where's Melvyn?

EVE: You 'aven't won yet, Lenny boy!

LINDA: Where's Melvyn?
  LINDA *takes up her position.*
  LEN *and another* MAN *appear.*

LEN: Come on, out the way! There's no point you sitting down in the middle of the track. We can easily move you. What's the matter with her?

MAN: What d'you mean what's the matter with her? She's having a baby.

LEN: Having a baby! She can't do! This airfield is government property. Get her out the way!

MAN: She's having a baby! You can't muck around with a woman when she's having a baby!

LINDA: Get Melvyn!

LEN: We gotta get the lorry out!

MAN: Well, you move her then. I'm not touching her.

LEN: Well, what we gonna do?

MAN: I don't know! Boil a kettle – or something.

LEN: Where are the rest of the men?

MAN: They're in the hut having a cuppa.

LEN: Go and get them. We'll carry the stuff past her.
  The MAN *goes off.*
  You don't think this is gonna stop me, do you? We are finishing today! Okay!
  MELVYN *arrives for work.*

MELVYN: What you going?

LINDA: Melvyn!
  He runs to her.

MELVYN: What you doing?

LINDA: Having the baby!

LEN: Get her out the way, Bragg! She's stopping the lorry getting out. She's deliberately blocking the road.

LINDA: He lied to us! They're finishing today!

MELVYN: Why? What for?

LINDA: So we'd ease up and not give 'em any trouble.

MELVYN: You see the thing is, Len, it's a woman's right to choose where to have her baby.

LEN: Not in the middle of my gate, it's not, Melvyn!

MELVYN: I think you're gonna just have to respect her decision.

LEN: All right, Bragg, you work for me! Get in the hut!

LINDA: Rub me back, Melvyn!
He does as he's told.

MELVYN: I won't be in today, Len. The wife's having a baby.
The MIDWIFE *arrives.*

MIDWIFE: What's going on, Linda?

LEN: Are you the nurse? Thank Christ! Tell her to move!

MIDWIFE: No I'm not! I'm the midwife. Get out the way!

MIDWIFE (*to* LINDA): Linda, you're down for a home birth. How long have you lived here?

LINDA: Val, you said if there were no complications you could have it in a field. Well here we are.

MIDWIFE: Two bowls, one bucket, a bed pan, a plastic sheet, a jug of sterile water and a nailbrush. Where are they?
The MAN *reappears.*

MAN: We've got an urn full of boiling water in the hut. If you want anything else just let me know.

MIDWIFE: I've no idea who you are but thank you very much. Right, it's a beautiful morning to be born, Linda, you're on! Let's see how much you're dilated.
The MIDWIFE *has a look.*

LEN: Where are the men?

MAN: In the hut having a cuppa.

LEN: Why aren't they out here?

MAN: We talked it over. And the feeling was, Melvyn is a good
worker, he's a good mate. His wife is having a baby. It's a
personal, family thing. There's no way we're gonna move her,
drive the lorry around her, or carry the stuff past her. And,
Len, your tea is getting cold

LEN *follows the* MAN *off.*

MIDWIFE: You're doing beautifully, Linda. You're three
centimetres dilated.

THE WOMEN *kneel round* LINDA. *The birth music begins.
The* MIDWIFE *talks us through.*

There are three stages of labour. The first stage pulls up and
opens the neck of the womb. The second stage is the journey
of the baby along the birth canal from the womb to the
outside world. The third stage is the delivery of the afterbirth.
The first stage is usually the longest and with a first baby takes
about ten hours on average. (*To audience:*) Don't worry we're
not going to keep you that long. In order to pull up and open
the mouth of the womb, the womb – which by the way is the
biggest muscle in the body and men haven't even got one – has
to contract. When it relaxes in between contractions it doesn't
go back to its original size it expands to a size slightly less
each time.

So the womb gradually gets smaller and smaller with each
contraction. At the height of the first stage of labour
contractions last about two minutes with about three minutes
off in between.

LINDA *has a contraction.*

Take a deep breath . . . that's it! Now as it gets stronger,
make your breathing shallower . . . Good! . . . Now just
breathe light and easy from the top of your chest! . . . Lovely!
And get deeper . . . And breathe normally again . . .
Tremendous! So as far as the baby is concerned, it's like being
inside a balloon that's slowly going down, being pushed
towards the opening. Inside the womb the baby is inside a sort
of plastic bag full of water. All this pushing and shoving
breaks the bag and at this point you and me get drenched,
Linda! Never mind!

Now when the mouth of the womb is wide open and the bag is

broken the contractions change from one's that open the womb to ones that push the baby out. They get stronger and come every one or two minutes. But you mustn't start pushing too soon, Linda. They've got to get nicely established before you can bear down. Don't push, darling! Wait till I tell you! How d'you feel?

LINDA: Sick as a dog.

MIDWIFE: It's a good sign, Linda. It means the womb's open and we're on the home straight.

So we're off on the second stage now. With every contraction Linda can help to push the baby a bit of the way along the birth canal. Maybe it'll take thirty minutes. Maybe it'll take two hours. The birth canal is curved. If she were flat on her back the baby would have to travel up hill. As it is gravity can do a bit of the work. She's pushed her baby's head into the vagina. It's starting to stretch the pelvic floor. It feels like her bum is going to burst. The head's almost at the opening of the vagina. The perineum is starting to be stretched. She's got a tearing sensation as if everything were splitting wide open.

LINDA *screams*.

Don't worry, Linda. You're fine! You're fine! I can see your baby's head. The head is coming. I can see the top of the head at the entrance to the vagina. Your baby's got its chin on its chest. And its going to lift up its head and put in its first appearance over the edge of the world. Here it comes. Don't rush it! Don't push! Pant! Pant! Pant! Lovely! Here it comes! The forehead! The nose! The little mouth! The chin! The whole head is out! Gently! Gently! We don't want any tearing! The head is turning as the shoulders turn. And the shoulders are out! And out come the hands and the trunk. You're all done, darling, you're all done. Hold your baby! Hold your baby!

LINDA: What is it?

MELVYN: It's a girl! It's a little girl!

LINDA *holds her baby on her stomach*.

You did it, Lin!

LINDA: Where's the lorry?

MELVYN: It hasn't moved.

LINDA: What about the men?

MELVYN: They went home hours ago.
   You did it! Everything!

LINDA: I did, didn't I.

EVE: Oh, she's beautiful, Lin! What you gonna call her?

LINDA: I'm gonna call her Eve.

EVE: Don't be silly! What you gonna call her?

LINDA: D'you mind! I'm gonna call her Eve!

EVE: I just thought you'd go for a nice name.

LINDA: It is a bloody nice name!

MIDWIFE: Right, I want to clamp and cut the cord and deliver the afterbirth.

EVE: Val, darling, don't get carried away. We don't have to go all through that. Let 'em look it up in a book when they get home.
   Right, now, ladies and gentlemen, I know you're all dying to have a little look and a cuddle. So can we first find someone to hold the baby while we do the finale? A real man to do a bit of baby-sitting, please?!
   She finds a male volunteer.
   She hasn't got a nappy on yet remember. Oh dear, never mind, it's lucky! Give her a kiss! . . . You're kissing the wrong end, love!

Out The Cord and Fly

Every day
You tell yourself
That there is nothing wrong

Then one day
You realise
You've lived the lie too long

Every day
You try to make
A life that is worthwhile

Then one day
It hits you hard
You've missed it by a mile

Kiss the old world bye-bye
Cut the cord and fly

Every day
You say okay
I'm just getting by

Then one day
You say no way
And look life in the eye

Every day
You build your wall
To hide the ugly view

Then one day
You meet someone
Who feels the same as you

And you say no
You've gotta go
Kiss the old world bye-bye
Cut the cord and fly.

Music for the Play

INTRO MUSIC

I'VE DONE IT

INTRO. Fast

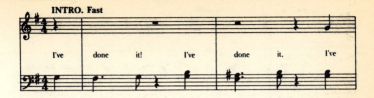

I've done it! I've done it, I've

done it, I've done it! oo ah

oo ah oo ah ba doo be doo bah! I've

ba doo be doo bah ba doo wa

VERSE

done it, I'm gon — na be a mum: I've

(Bass words same time each verse)

ba doowah ba doo wa ba doo wah ba doo wa

fal — len, my ov – en's got a bun: I've

ba doo wa ba doo wa ba doo wah ba doo wa

I'VE DONE IT (cont.)

SITTING IN THE CLINIC

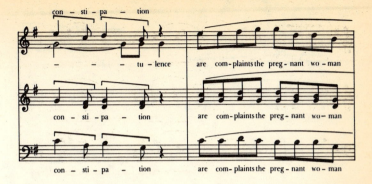

don't for — get that it — chy, twit — chy hae — mor — rhoid Yes, be — ing

don't for — get that it — chy, twit — chy hae — mor — rhoid Yes, be — ing

don't for — get that it — chy, twit — chy hae — mor — rhoíd Yes, be — ing

1st and 2nd times

preg nant's so much fun, life is ni — cer as a nun

preg nant's so much fun, life is ni — cer as a nun

preg nant's so much fun, life is ni — cer as a nun as a nun,

Da CAPO (verse 2.)

final time

let's all be — come one! A — men

let's all be — come one! A — men

let's all be — come one! A — men

Fine:

WOMAN'S WORK

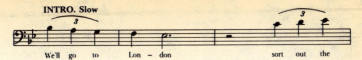

INTRO. Slow

We'll go to Lon – don ... sort out the

gov – ern – ment ... You stay in Brad – stow

sort out a – bout be – ing a mum cos there's no

½ CHORUS
Faster tempo

clash of i – de – o – lo – gy ___ between po – li – tics and bi –

– o – lo – gy ___ cos its all woman's work and woman's

WOMAN'S WORK (cont.)

Fine:

WOMAN'S WORK (cont.)

'cos there's no *etc.*

'cos there's no *etc.*

we'll go to Lon - don

ba ba da da

FULL CHORUS

sort out the go - vern - ment

you stay in

m ba ba da da

ba ba da da

m ba ba da da

Brad - stow

sort out a -

ba ba da da

m ba ba da da

bout

be - ing a mum 'cos there's no

da

To ½ CHORUS

ANOTHER WOMAN GOES

-oth-er wo-man goes   as an-oth-er wo-man goes...

CHORUS
Faster

Yes she still loves him and she

she loves him she loves him

ba ba ba ba ba ba ba doo ba ba doo ba ba

still wants him__ no she can-not stay__ she's got ta

She loves him she can't stay she can't stay she's got to

doo, ba ba doo, ba ba doo, ba ba doo; ba ba

ANOTHER WOMAN GOES (cont.)

ANOTHER WOMAN GOES (cont.)

Is she lo — — sing or is she win —

Is she lo — — — —

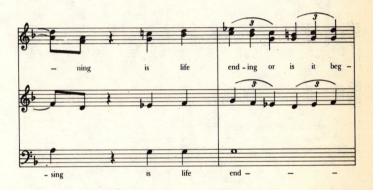

— ning is life end-ing or is it beg —

— sing is life end — — —

in — ning?

Slowing

as an — o —ther wo — man goes ___

Fine:

— — ing?

I'VE HAD ENOUGH

dop   dwee oo da   n   dop *etc.*

(nough)

VERSE

tell you lit – tle sto–ry   'bout a   woman who travelled down south

qui – et lit – tle la – dy   didn't   like to   op-en her mouth

well

dop   dwee oo da   dwee   oo da   dop

CHORUS

I'VE HAD ENOUGH (cont.)

well   this   wo – man gets   go – ing   when the
dop

last time

go – ing   gets   tough   I've   had e –   nough

LABOUR WARD ONE-O-NINE

LABOUR WARD ONE-O-NINE (cont.)

ba - by's __ Pa: they shaved our pu — bic hair be — fore he'd

parked the car, and then they caught us nap – ping with the

e – ne – ma, do we have one hell of a.

time! ____ Find your - self the two girls with the

loud - est _____ scream: you can bet the bed you get is

in be - tween.   I   hate to think what's go - ing on be -

hind that screen,   do   we   have one hell of a

We're _ the   wo - men _____   in mat -

time! _____   the wo - men _____

- er – ni – ty

mat – er – ni – ty the girls on La-bour Ward One O Nine

O Nine. We love, we

num–ber num–ber num–ber num–ber One O___ Nine we

love it, and e – ven though we're not sick we would-n't

miss it. (you'll al – ways find us here) Come on and

LABOUR WARD ONE-O-NINE (cont.)

join us. Just find a fel – low and click, you can

come! come back al – most each and ev' ry sin – gle year.

2nd time

p

in ma-

O Nine, we're the wo – men the wo – men

One O_____ Nine

- ter – ni – ty

mat – er – ni – ty, the girls on La-bour Ward One O Nine

pp

One O Nine!

pp

I'VE CHANGED

have to break the law to find you're in the wrong it's

we've all changed and let me tell you how___

just a diff-rent vis-ion from the pow'rs that be, and soon it's

we've all changed tell you we've all changed___

spoken

gone what's it called?

I guess a

pret-ty soon it's miss-ing, oo oo dem – o – cra-cy

lot of peo-ple have known it __ all the time but I

we've all changed tell you we've all changed __

real - ly thought this coun - try could hear a voice like mine

we've all changed and let me tell you how __

now I've start - ed look ing and it's plain to see __ who runs the

we've all changed, tell you we've all changed __

MOVE OVER MAMA (cont.)

CHORUS (very smooth)

Move o - ver mam-ma   I   need some el - bow room

(suggested solo if you get fed up with doubling bass)

mam ma mam ma

Move o - ver mam - ma ma' move o - ver mam-ma, ma'

move o - ver mam ma, need some space in - side this womb.

move__ o - ver mam ma ma ma move, ma ma move mama mam ma.

move o - ver mam ma, ma' move ov - er mam ma, ma'

Move o - ver mam ma __ you're gon na have to choose if you

move__ o - ver mam ma, you're gon - na have to choose

move o - ver mam ma, ma' move o - ver mam ma, mam ma

MOVE OVER MAMA

Once I had a bo—dy, it was mine, all mine___

did what I told it most of the time___

most of the time___

Then my ba—by moved in, made him self at home___

now a days my bo—dy ain't my own

changed, I've got a ve ry alt ered out look, I'm

we've all changed tell you we've all changed we're

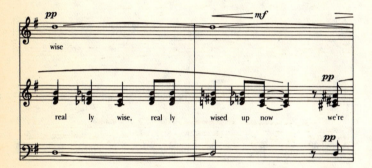

wise

real ly wise, real ly wised up now we're

I've real ly wised up now. Yeah!

real ly wise real ly wised up now Yeah!

Fine:

MOVE OVER MAMA (cont.)

Want a ba—by, got to pay your ba—by dues

move ba by dues

ba, ba ba! ba, ba ba

doo doo doo doo doo doo

VERSE II & III

Talk-ing 'bout your di—et, think it on—ly best

doo ba ba doo doo ba doo ba ba doo doo ba

I'll eat all the good stuff, you can have the rest

need me, feed me.

Doo ba ba doo doo ba

MOVE OVER MAMA (cont.)

make no bones with-out it, I'm a low down thief___ if

Doo ba ba doo doo ba doo ba ba doo doo ba,

you don't score me cal—cium, I'll take all your teeth!

doo ba ba doo doo ba; all your teeth!
(or equivalent last 3 words)

VERSE IV

Take me to the clin—ic, doc will see you now___

doo ba da doo doo ba doo ba ba doo doo ba

tell him how you're feel-ing, like a Preg-nant cow___

tell him, tell him!

doo ba ba doo doo ba

climb up on the scales and roll up both your sleeves ___ un -
Doo ba ba doo doo ba doo ba ba doo doo ba

- dress be – hind the cur- tain, lie on the couch, o – pen wide
doo ba ba doo doo,

take a deep breath, say ah! smile and pass a ur- ine sam-ple please!

To CHORUS (last time)

LEAFLET

doom doom doom *etc.*

doom doom doom *etc*

Fine last time

gloom   gloom   doom

please ac – cept this leaf – let it's a

please   ac   –   cept this leaf – let

ter – ri – fy – ing read it' – ll   scare the shit right from you

it's   quite   ter – ri – fy – ing   it   will   scare you

might

ne – ver   choose to breed

Come on take my leaf – let   it

come   on   take my leaf – let

on – ly says you'll die   won't you face the night-mare you

it   on – ly says you'll die   won't you face the night-mare

must – n't be so shy   oh there's al – ways some guy say – ing

oh!

some – thing nas – ty's go – ing on   some one some – where's do – ing some such

The whole world's go – ing wrong   if you ev – er stopped and pond ered

oh

ev - ery thingthat this guy said

you are just a sim - ple fel - lah

it would des - troy your bleed -ing head

doom doom doom *etc.*

LET'S TAKE THE TRAIN

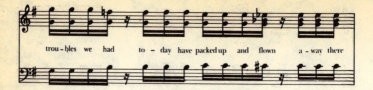

trou – bles we had to – day have packed up and flown a – way there

is – n't a cloud in the whole darn ____ sky

Let's take the train home you and ____ I deal out

Those cards, my luck is rid – ing high: owe a

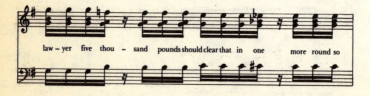

law – yer five thou – sand pounds should clear that in one more round so

Let's take the train home, you and I, be – cause we've

Let's take the train home, you and I, be – cause we've

1st time

won, we've won, we've won our case: we've won our case today I said we've

won, we've won, we've etc.

won, yes we've won, yes we've, etc.

won won won won

DAL SEGNO (VERSE II)

won, we've won, we've won our case, and a whole new life be – gins to – day

and a whole new life be – gins to – day

ba ba

3

LET'S TAKE THE TRAIN (cont.)

won our case we won our case we've

won our case we won we

won our case we won our case we
won hip hip hoo – ray!
be doo, doo doo

LAST TIME

Let's take the train home you and___ I if we're
dm   dm   dm   dm ba   ba

___ to – geth- er, sis – ter we'll get by lean

on me cos that's O. K. I'm right with you all the way, the

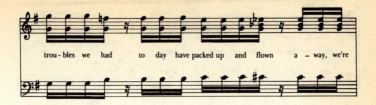

trou - bles we had to day have packed up and flown a – way, we're

ty – ing one on to night that man of mine's seen the light so

let's take the train home let's take the train home

you, and I
da da da da da da da yeah
yeah

Fine:

TODAY'S THE DAY

VERSE I & III
Quite fast

Oh!   I got a   low back___ pain it's sort of

.. oo _____ and here it comes a – gain___

oh!

tell you ho – ney ain't no doubt   what goes in must come right on out

oh!

pack my   case is the   car O. K?

___   is the car O.

TODAY'S THE DAY (cont.)

phone the nurse 'cos to day's ── the day to – day's the

K.

to – day to – day to – day to –

CHORUS

day I've wait – ed for a day not

day is the day to – day, to – day is the day to – day to –

like a – ny oth – er I'm star – ry

day a day not like a – ny oth – er to –

eyed I'm pet – ri – fied and I'm

day is the day to – day to – day is the day to – day to –

TODAY'S THE DAY (cont.)

going to be a mo – ther   yes, in – deed!

day   Fine:

VERSE II (Chorus tacet)

Eve loved Ad – am on __ day ____ one

nine months lat – er she had a son __

oh! __

who needs an ap – ple ____ who needs a snake?

oh! __

we're all still mak – ing ____ the same ____ mis – take

TODAY'S THE DAY (cont.)

pack my ___ case is the car ___ O. K?

is the car O.

To CHORUS

phone the nurse, ___ 'cos to – day's ___ the day to – day's the

K?

to – day, to – day to – day to –

THE BIRTH

Midwife: You're doing beautifully Linda,
You're three centimetres dilated.

until: 'men haven't even got one'

ha ha ha *etc.*

Men   haven't got one   haven't got one

until:
'about three minutes off in between'

Linda:

into scream

Ahoo!

until: 'never mind'

until:
'every one or two minutes'

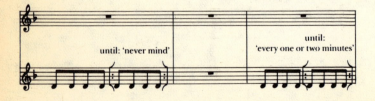

THE BIRTH (cont.)

THE BIRTH (cont.)

until:
'over the edge of the world'

la *etc.*

la la la la la la   la!

Fine:

CUT THE CHORD

there is no – thing wrong | there is no – thing

no – thing wrong
no — thing wrong _____ | there's no – thing _____

then one day_____ you re – al – ize _____ you've

_____ you re – al — ize | you've
wrong you re – al – ize _____ you've

lived the lie too long _____

lived the lie too | long _____

lived the lie too long | lived the lie too
lived the lie too | long ev – ery day__